SCHOLASTIC

BEST PRACTICES *in Action*

Fluency Practice
Read-Aloud Plays

GRADES 1-2

BY KATHLEEN M. HOLLENBECK

NEW YORK • TORONTO • LONDON • AUCKLAND • SYDNEY
MEXICO CITY • NEW DELHI • HONG KONG • BUENOS AIRES

Teaching *Resources*

To Lyn Bernadyn

and Carolyn Kullberg,

whose commitment and expertise

never fail to inspire.

Cover design by Brian LaRossa
Interior design by Kathy Massaro
Interior art by Bari Weissman

ISBN–13: 978-0-439-55419-0
ISBN–10: 0-439-55419-5

4   5   6   7   8   9   10   40   14   13   12   11

Contents

INTRODUCTION

*f*luency, the ability to decode words quickly and accurately, is more than just a buzzword in education. It is a fundamental skill that must be achieved in order for readers to find meaning in words.

Oral reading offers tremendous insight into a student's level of fluency. The fluent reader glides through text almost effortlessly, reading with meaning, expression, and appropriate pacing. A struggling reader labors over words, deciphering them in a slow, halting manner that hinders comprehension.

Training and practice are essential to achieving reading fluency, and oral reading offers an unmatched opportunity for both. *Read-Aloud Plays for Building Fluency: Grades 1–2* provides 15 oral reading opportunities that make reading practice easy, entertaining, and rewarding. The plays explore topics from core-curricular areas and adhere to national standards for first and second grades.

In addition to the plays, inside this book you'll find activities to strengthen skills in fluency, phonics, and oral reading; a section devoted to enhancing the Readers Theater experience (see Using Readers Theater, page 16); and tools for assessment, including a teacher rubric and a checklist students can use to guide and monitor their own reading progress (see Assessing Fluency, page 9). The plays and activities target specific skills designed to increase word recognition, decoding accuracy, use of expression, and ultimately, comprehension—the primary goal of reading instruction.

The text adheres to vocabulary standards based on the studies of Harris and Jacobson. These standards ensure that your students will encounter words contained in the first- and second-grade reading vocabularies rather than those that might hinder their progress.

The text of each play has been leveled using readability scores from the Lexile Framework for Reading (see chart, page 14). These scores offer guidelines to help you select the scripts that best match the needs and reading levels of each student. The plays are ready for use to practice, strengthen, and assess skills in reading fluency. And they all share the same objective: to give students practice reading comfortably, confidently, and with enthusiasm, helping to build an ever-growing flock of fluent readers within the walls of your classroom.

Fluency: An Overview

What Is Fluency?

Fluency is the mark of a proficient reader. When a student reads text quickly, gets most of the words right, and uses appropriate expression and phrasing, we say that he or she has achieved fluency. Fluency frees readers from the struggle that slows them down. Hence, they are able to read for meaning and to understand. They can attend to the details of text, pausing as indicated and varying tone and pace to enhance comprehension for both themselves and potential listeners.

How Does Fluency Develop?

As with every skill worth developing, fluency sharpens with experience. Exposure to print, immersion in a rich linguistic environment, and practice, practice, practice all lead to fluent reading.

From the emergent on up, readers must learn and apply tools to help them advance. The National Institute for Literacy (NIFL) speaks of fluency as a skill in flux.

> "Fluency is not a stage of development at which readers can read all words quickly and easily. Fluency changes, depending on what readers are reading, their familiarity with the words, and the amount of their practice with reading text. Even very skilled readers may read in a slow, labored manner when reading texts with many unfamiliar words or topics." (NIFL, 2001)

Readers are most comfortable (and most fluent) when reading what they have seen before or what they know most about. When venturing beyond these areas, they must rely on word attack skills, prior knowledge, and the host of tools that have helped them advance to this point.

Ways to Build Fluency

Two words encompass what readers require for the development of fluency: *exposure* and *practice*. To foster fluent reading, be sure to:

✳ **MODEL FLUENT READING.** Read aloud to students. As you read, model (and point out) aspects of fluent reading such as phrasing, pacing, and expression. Help students understand that people aren't born knowing how to do this; they learn it by hearing it and trying it themselves.

> "Fluent readers read aloud effortlessly and with expression. Their reading sounds natural, as if they are speaking. Readers who have not yet developed fluency read slowly, word by word. Their oral reading is choppy and plodding."
>
> NATIONAL INSTITUTE FOR LITERACY, 2001

✳ **PROVIDE STUDENTS WITH PLENTY OF READING PRACTICE.** Oral reading is highly effective for tracking and strengthening fluency. It enables both the reader and the listener to hear the reader and assess progress, and it allows the listener to provide guidance as needed. Whisper reading serves as a transition from oral to silent reading. In whisper reading, all students read aloud at the same time, but at a volume that is just barely audible. The student is able to self-monitor, and the teacher can move around the room, noting progress, keeping students on task, and offering guidance as needed. For silent reading, students read an assigned passage or a book of their own choice. Because the reader cannot be heard, assessment of reading skill is not possible. The value of silent reading is that it increases time spent reading and gives students "opportunities to expand and practice reading strategies" (Fountas and Pinnell, 2001).

✳ **SELECT APPROPRIATE TEXT.** To develop fluency, a student must practice reading text at his or her independent reading level—the level at which he or she is able to accurately decode 96 to 100 percent of the words in a given text. This level varies for every student. By assessing each student's reading level up front, you will be prepared to select appropriate texts and ensure that your students get a lot of practice reading at a level at which they achieve success (Rasinski, 2003; Worthy and Broaddus, 2001/2002). For information about how to use text to assess fluency, see Assessing Fluency, page 9.

✳ **RAISE THE BAR.** Read aloud to students from text that is above their independent reading level, exposing them to new and more difficult words and concepts without the pressure of having to decode.

✳ **GIVE ROOM TO GROW.** To help a student advance in fluency, present text at his or her instructional level. This text can be read with 90 to 95 percent accuracy. With a little help, the student can get almost all the words right (Blevins, 2001a; Rasinski, 2003).

✳ **PROVIDE DIRECT INSTRUCTION AND FEEDBACK.** Prepare students before they read. First review phonics skills they will need to decode words. Draw attention to sight words, root words, affixes, and word chunks. Preteach difficult or unfamiliar words. Demonstrate the use of intonation, phrasing, and expression, and tell children when they have done these well. Listen to children read, and offer praise as well as helpful tips for the next attempt.

✳ **USE A VARIETY OF READING MATERIALS.** In addition to the plays included in this book, fiction stories, nonfiction passages, and poetry offer a rich and varied reading experience. Expose your students to each of these. Give them many opportunities to get excited about and immerse themselves in what they are reading.

* **HIGHLIGHT PHRASING.** One of the most effective ways to help students who are struggling with fluency is to use phrase-cued text. Phrase-cued text is marked by slashes to indicate where readers should pause. One slash indicates a pause or meaningful chunk of text within a sentence. Two slashes indicate a longer pause at the end of a sentence. Ready-made samples of phrase-cued text are available (see Resources for Reading Fluency, Comprehension, and Readers Theater, page 21), but you can also convert any passage of text to phrase-cued text by reading it aloud, listening for pauses and meaningful chunks of text, and drawing slashes in the appropriate places. (See the example, below, from the play "Bear Cub Comes Home," page 30.) Model fluent reading with proper phrasing and invite students to practice with the text you have marked.

Narrator :	The little cub/ walked and walked.// He came/ to a forest.
Bear Cub:	I am/ very sleepy.// I will/ lie down/ and rest.// I will/ look for/ my home/ tomorrow.//

Bringing Oral Reading into Your Classroom

Provide opportunities for children to read aloud. This may include any or all of the following:

* **INTERACTIVE READ-ALOUD:** An adult reader demonstrates fluent oral reading and talks about how he or she changes tone, pace, or expression in response to the play, story, or poem. Students enjoy a dramatic reading and absorb skills in fluent reading. In addition, the interactive read-aloud provides an opportunity for teachers to ask open-ended questions before, during, and after the reading, soliciting students' prior knowledge and extending their understanding, comprehension, and connection with the topic. This connection can advance student interaction with the text and promote optimal conditions for fluency.

* **SHARED READING:** An adult reader models fluent reading and then invites children to read along, using Big Books or small-group instruction.

* **CHORAL READING:** An adult and children read aloud together. This activity works especially well with poetry and cumulative tales.

* **ECHO READING:** A child repeats phrases or sentences read by someone else, mimicking tone, expression, and pacing.

> "Students who are having trouble with comprehension may not be putting words together in meaningful phrases or chunks as they read. Their oral reading is characterized by a choppy, word-by-word delivery that impedes comprehension. These students need instruction in phrasing written text into appropriate segments."
>
> (BLEVINS, 2001A)

* **REPEATED READING:** An adult reads aloud while a student listens and then reads again while the student follows along. Then the adult invites the student to read along, and finally, the student reads the same text aloud alone. This technique is most helpful for struggling readers.

* **PAIRED REPEATED READING:** Teachers group students in pairs, matching above-level readers with on-level readers and on-level readers with those below level. Partners are encouraged to take turns reading aloud to each other, each reading a short passage three times and then getting feedback. The manner of grouping provides every struggling reader with a more proficient reader to model.

* **READERS THEATER:** Students work in groups to rehearse and perform one or more plays from this book. Performing can be exciting, and the drive to present well can be a powerful force behind mastering fluency in reading and speech, motivating both struggling and proficient readers. (For more about Readers Theater, including activities for building fluency, see page 16.)

* **TAPE-ASSISTED READING:** Children listen to books on tape while reading along in a book. (Consider recording your own tapes if commercially made tapes go too quickly, or if the tapes include background elements, such as music or sound effects, which can be distracting.) Children can also listen to and critique their own reading on tape.

* **PHRASE-CUED TEXT:** See Highlight Phrasing, page 7.

Where Does Vocabulary Fit In?

Stumbling over words constitutes one of the main setbacks on the way to fluency. It remains in your students' best interest, then, to grow familiar with words they will likely encounter in reading. Cunningham and Allington (2003) urge active use of word walls, inviting student participation in choosing words to put on the walls, eliminating words rarely used, and reviewing the list of words daily.

Enhancing Comprehension

In all reading instruction, it is important to remember that reading imparts meaning, and so the fundamental goal of reading is to comprehend. All other instruction—phonics, phonemic awareness, auditory discrimination—is wasted effort if comprehension gets lost in the process. Consequently, those who find no purpose or meaning in the written word will soon lose interest in reading it altogether. Avoid this by teaching your students strategies to enhance comprehension. Help them learn to question the text they are reading. *What is the message? Does it make sense to them? Do they know what it means?* Find out by asking questions. Ask questions before students read, to prepare them for the play. Ask as they read, to deepen their understanding of the text. Ask additional questions after they read, to clear up any comprehension issues and summarize the play. Teach your students to formulate questions of their own to give them a vested interest in what they are reading.

Assessing Fluency

There are two ways to assess a student's progress in fluency: informally and formally. Informal assessment involves listening to students read aloud, noting how easily, quickly, and accurately they read, and deciding how well they attend to phrasing, expression, and other elements. Formal assessment involves timing a student's oral reading to create a tangible record of his or her progress throughout the school year.

To conduct an informal assessment of students' reading fluency, use the reproducible Teacher Rubric for Oral Reading Fluency on page 10. Have a student read aloud for five to seven minutes while you note on the form the strategies the student uses as well as his or her reading strengths and difficulties.

Students can monitor their own progress using the Student Checklist for Self-Assessment on page 11. Photocopy and laminate this form for each student. Review the checklist components with students many times, until they understand the purpose of the checklist and the meaning of each statement. Encourage students to mentally complete the checklist from time to time to track their own reading fluency.

To carry out what is called timed repeated reading, select a passage of text (150–200 words) that is at the student's independent reading level and that he or she has never read before. Have the student read aloud the passage for one minute. Track your own copy of the text while he or she reads, marking words omitted or pronounced incorrectly. Count the number of words the student read correctly. Then give the student three one-minute opportunities (in separate sessions) to read the same text, and average the scores to obtain his or her oral reading fluency rate.*

In Conclusion

Does fluency instruction work? Research has shown that concentrated reading instruction can dramatically improve reading comprehension and fluency, which in turn affect academic performance, self-esteem, and overall achievement. With this in mind, it is not only helpful to instruct with an eye toward fluency, it is essential.

> "Instruction that focuses too heavily on word-perfect decoding sends a message that good reading is nothing more than accurate word recognition. As a result, students tend to shoot for accuracy at the expense of everything else, including meaning."
>
> (RASINSKI, 2004)

---

* For more detailed information on timed reading, consult Blevins (2001a, pp. 9–12) and Rasinski (2003, pp. 82–83).

Teacher Rubric for Oral Reading Fluency

Child's Name: _____ Date: _____

Grade: _____ Passage: _____

For each category, circle the number that best describes the student's performance.

Accuracy

4	Recognizes most words; works to pronounce unfamiliar words, repeating them to self-correct if necessary.
3	Recognizes most words; works to pronounce unfamiliar words, self-correcting if necessary; sometimes requires assistance.
2	Struggles to decode and decipher words; hesitates before attempting to pronounce new words; usually requires assistance.
1	Recognizes very few words; makes no attempt to pronounce unfamiliar words.

Expression and Volume

4	Uses expression and volume that is natural to conversational language and that varies according to the content of the text.
3	Uses expression and volume that is appropriate to conversational language and the content of the text; sometimes hesitates when unsure of text.
2	Often speaks softly and in a monotone; pays little attention to expression or volume; focuses on getting through the text.
1	Reads words in a monotone and in a quiet voice.

Phrasing

4	Groups words into meaningful phrases or chunks of text.
3	Usually groups words into meaningful phrases or chunks of text.
2	Reads primarily in groups of two or three words.
1	Reads word by word without meaning.

Pace

4	Reads at a suitable pace and responds to punctuation with appropriate pausing and intonation.
3	Usually reads at a suitable pace and attends to most punctuation with appropriate pausing and intonation; halts at times when unsure.
2	Reads slowly, sometimes two or three words at a time; halts often; pays little attention to punctuation or pacing.
1	Reads words slowly in a string; does not heed punctuation.

Prosody

4	Attends to the rhythm of language, reading comfortably and without hesitating or halting.
3	Occasionally halts or runs sentences together when challenged by words or sentence structure.
2	Reads smoothly at times but most often slowly.
1	Reading sounds stilted and unnatural and lacks meaning.

Source: Adapted from "Training Teachers to Attend to Their Students' Oral Reading Fluency," by J. Zutell and T. V. Rasinski, 1991, *Theory Into Practice 30*, pp. 211–217. Used with permission of the authors. ● *Fluency Practice Read-Aloud Plays: Grades 1–2* Scholastic Teaching Resources

Name: _____

How Carefully Do I Read?

	Most of the Time	Sometimes	Hardly Ever
1 I say a word again if it does not sound right.	☐	☐	☐
2 I pay attention to punctuation at the end of a sentence.	☐	☐	☐
3 I try to read without stopping after every word.	☐	☐	☐
4 I read with expression.	☐	☐	☐
5 I am ready to speak when it is my turn.	☐	☐	☐

What I Need to Work on:

_____

_____

_____

_____

Adapted from *35 Rubrics & Checklists to Assess Reading and Writing* by Adele Fiderer. Permission to reuse granted by the author.
Fluency Practice Read-Aloud Plays: Grades 1–2   Scholastic Teaching Resources

Using the Plays to Enhance Fluency

A Fluency Mini-Lesson

Let this sample mini-lesson serve as a model for using the plays to strengthen and assess reading fluency. The mini-lesson may be conducted with small groups or with the class as a whole.

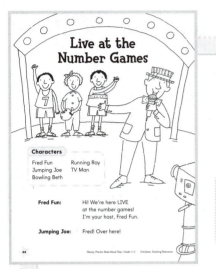

READ-ALOUD PLAY 7

Live at the Number Games

PREPARATION: Give each child a copy of the play "Live at the Number Games" (pages 44–47). Note: For this model lesson, give students a copy of the same play. As they become more fluent, select different plays for each group to rehearse and perform.

Prereading

1. Introduce unfamiliar or difficult words children will come across in the text, such as *host* and *watch* as well as some of the more complex high-use words: *number, about,* and *good-bye.* Help children decode the words. Review them several times to aid recognition and boost fluency. (See Preparing for Difficult or Unfamiliar Text, page 15, for more about the vocabulary in the plays.)

2. Review reading techniques that promote fluency, such as reading from left to right, "smooshing" words together, and crossing the page with a steady, sweeping eye movement. (Blevins, 2001a)

3. Divide the class into small groups, equal in size to the number of characters in the play.

Reading and Modeling

1. Depending on the children's level of reading proficiency, you may want to read the play aloud and then invite the group to read along with you. As you read, point out ways in which your pacing, intonation, and expression lend meaning to the text. You might ask:

"Did you notice how my voice rose at the end of the sentence 'That hole is five feet long!'? That's what we do when we see an exclamation point. We know the sentence tells something exciting; we use our voices to make it sound that way."

Fred Fun:	It's Jumping Joe!
Jumping Joe:	I am about to jump over this hole in the sand.
Fred Fun:	That hole is five feet long! Can you jump that far?
Jumping Joe:	Watch me!
(Joe jumps.)	
Fred Fun:	Wow! That was some jump!
Jumping Joe:	I jumped five feet! Am I good or what?
Bowling Beth:	Fred! Over here!
Fred Fun:	It's Bowling Beth!
Bowling Beth:	I am about to tip over ten pins with one ball.
Fred Fun:	Can you do that?

45

Bowling Beth:	Watch me!
(She rolls the ball. Ten pins fall.)	
Fred Fun:	Wow! You did it!
Bowling Beth:	Ten pins! Am I good or what?
Running Ray:	Fred! Over here!
Fred Fun:	It's Running Ray!
Running Ray:	I am about to run one mile in seven minutes.
Fred Fun:	Can you run that fast?
Running Ray:	Watch me!
(He runs and runs.)	
Fred Fun:	You did it!
Running Ray:	Seven minutes! Am I good or what?

46

TV Man:	Fred Fun! Over here!
Fred Fun:	It's my boss!
TV Man:	We have two seconds left in our show. You need to say good-bye, Fred.
Fred Fun:	Well, this ends our time at the Number Games! Tune in next week when we go to the Letter Limbo!

✳ THE END ✳

47

---

2. Try reading the sentences without the inflection. Observe aloud that exclamatory sentences read without the appropriate tone sound flat and stilted, without depth, character, or expression.

3. Then point out other punctuation marks that require voice or tone changes, such as the question mark in *Can you run that fast?* and the period in *I am about to run one mile in seven minutes.*

4. Read the play aloud again, inviting children to read aloud with you as they are able. Note: If you feel that a group of readers is already proficient, preview the words and then have the children read the play aloud without modeling.

5. Once readers have read the play several times, go back and emphasize aspects of phonics and vocabulary that will increase their understanding of language, encourage fast, accurate reading, and deepen comprehension. (You may want to write some specific lines from the play on sentence strips and use a pocket chart to manipulate words and phrases.) "Live at the Number Games" presents opportunities to explore such topics as:

✳ **contractions:** *I'm, It's*

✳ **number words and time-related words:** *one, two, five, seven, ten, seconds.* Have students underline all the number words and time-related words in the play.

✳ **phrasing:** Readers must pause after all ending punctuation. They will pause for a shorter time between the two sentences that follow one after the other and are meant to be read more quickly, such as: *Wow! You did it!* and *Seven minutes! Am I good or what?*

✳ **homonyms:** *two, to*

(Fluency techniques such as echo reading and choral reading work especially well with repetitive verse. "Three Nice Mice," page 24, and "Bear Cub Comes Home," page 30, offer text well-suited for exploring these methods.)

Play Readability Scores

The chart below shows the readability scores of the plays in this collection. The texts were leveled using the Lexile Framework for Reading. These scores offer guidelines to help you select the plays that best match the needs and reading levels of each student. For more information about the Lexile Framework, go to www.lexile.com. (See Preparing for Difficult or Unfamiliar Text, page 15, for more about the vocabulary in the plays.)

Play Title	Lexile Score*
1. Three Nice Mice	BR
2. Who Needs a Fan?	BR
3. Bear Cub Comes Home	BR
4. The Last Apple	10L
5. The Sun Will Come	20L
6. I'm First!	70L
7. Live at the Number Games	80L
8. Polly Learns to Swim	120L
9. Babe Ruth	160L
10. Bella and Jade	160L
11. Betsy Ross	200L
12. Chicken Tricks	210L
13. Cats Care for Their Kittens	230L
14. Hide and Go Seek!	230L
15. Little Puppy	250L

BR = Beginning Reader

* The Lexile score is based on dialogue text only. Conventional play formatting (such as the names that indicate which character is speaking) was removed during the scoring process.

A Lexile Score of **BR to 250** is appropriate for the first-grade independent reading level.
A Lexile Score of **150 to 350** is appropriate for the second-grade independent reading level.

Please note: The most difficult play scores at 100 Lexiles below the recommended maximum. This has been done to offset additional difficulty that emergent and early readers might encounter when reading stage directions and character names.

Preparing for Difficult or Unfamiliar Text

To assess fluency, have children read text that is new to them (Blevins, 2001a). With this in mind, when using the plays for assessment, do not prepare students by introducing unfamiliar or difficult words. Prereading may distort the assessment results.

Before reading for the purpose of *developing* fluency, however, it is helpful to highlight words that may prove to be stumbling blocks for young or struggling readers. Words slightly above grade level, difficult words on grade level, and complex high-frequency words can be daunting when encountered for the first time within text. To prevent this, introduce words and help children decode them before they read. Give them a chance to decipher the words before you provide correct pronunciation. Then review the words several times to aid recognition and boost fluency.

The following words may be unfamiliar or challenging to your students. Some are within the common first- and second-grade vocabulary but may contain difficult or unfamiliar letter patterns. Others have been categorized as common to text read by slightly older readers (Harris and Jacobsen, 1982). These words were selected for use in the plays when necessary to enhance the flow of the text or where substitutions would not carry the same meaning, such as the word *cheese* in the play "Three Nice Mice," page 24. Note that character names are not included in the unfamiliar vocabulary words listed below. Review characters' names with children before they read.

Three Nice Mice
three, turns, milk, cheese

Who Needs a Fan?
bright, plan, wind, windy

Bear Cub Comes Home
bear, walk, where, forest, tomorrow

The Last Apple
apples, everywhere, drop, climbed, catch, somehow

The Sun Will Come
mouse, wind, blew, pretty, clouds, morning, bright

I'm First!
first, always, walk, pretty, leaves, friends, lost

Live at the Number Games
host, sand, watch, what, minutes, seconds, Letter Limbo

Polly Learns to Swim
penguins, splashed, without, chicks, scared, swimming, afraid, feathers, flippers, through

Babe Ruth
teachers, throw, catch, twelve, join, baseball players

Bella and Jade
garden, leave, caterpillar, tomorrow, hungry, sweet, different, butterfly

Betsy Ross
grandmother, hundred, United States, country, sewing, General, flags, anything, started, stripes, beautiful

Chicken Tricks
chicken, tricks, fooled, wind, stepped, fence, field, ideas, scared, board, listened, toward

Cats Care for Their Kittens
kittens, licking, cleaning, milk, drink, mouth, themselves

Hide and Go Seek!
bright, quickly, moss, stick, climb, leaves, finished, around, ground, agree, favorite, branch, noise

Little Puppy
itty-bitty, pretty, listen, ruff, treat, twice, unhappy, friends

Using Readers Theater

Readers Theater offers children a fun, interactive way to build fluency. By reading, rehearsing, and performing scripts at their independent reading levels, children learn to navigate and use the written word in exciting, amusing, and purposeful ways. Readers Theater motivates children to experiment with language, working with expression, pacing, tone, inflection, meaning, and interpretation. As they take part in Readers Theater, children step out of the basal and into a world of language and meaning brought to life.

Tips for Building Fluency with Readers Theater

● Limit Props

Props can distract young readers and hinder the success of fluent reading. If you do choose to include props, be sure they are simple and easy to hold. Since scripts are meant to be read aloud rather than memorized, it is important that every reader has one hand free to hold the script.

● Treat Scripts as Stories

With the purpose of building strong readers ever in sight, treat the text of a play in much the same way as the text of a Big Book, a poem, or a story. Read the title with students. Anticipate what the play might be about, and predict outcomes, conflicts, and character behaviors. Invite students to tell how they feel about the plot of the play. See A Fluency Mini-Lesson, page 12, for more ideas on using the plays to boost reading skills.

● Heed Clues for Direction

Help students recognize hints in both stage directions and dialogue text that indicate physical movement as well as the pitch, emotion, or volume of speech. For example, words spelled in all capital letters are generally intended to be shouted. Stage directions often indicate not only activity (*He runs and runs*) but appropriate tone of voice (for example, *crossly*).

Develop Prosody

Prosody, or the rhythm of language, comes alive in Readers Theater—but only when readers are able to read their text easily. Children need to read and reread their scripts many times in order to feel comfortable reading their own character's lines and understanding the purpose and flow of the play. Encourage readers to work first in pairs, and then in small groups and individually, to practice the text until they feel comfortable reading it aloud. This will make for a smoother performance—and a more confident, capable reader!

Consider Placement

When performing Readers Theater, it's effective for children to stand so they can be seen and heard. Have readers face the person(s) to whom they are speaking, and have the narrator speak directly to the audience. It works well to have all performers "onstage" at once, standing in a semi-circle and facing the audience. As your students grow with Readers Theater, movement and staging can be added to the performance, if desired.

Using Language Clues To Develop a Strong Performance

Attend to Punctuation

Emphasize the impact of ending punctuation. Model and then invite students to say the same sentence three different ways, using a period, a question mark, and an exclamation point. For example, from "Polly Learns to Swim," page 48, you might read the sentence *She walked over ice and snow* as follows:

※ "She walked over ice and snow."

※ "She walked over ice and snow?"

※ "She walked over ice and snow!"

Explore Dialogue

Draw attention toward using dialogue to represent each character's unique personality. For example, in the play "Babe Ruth," page 52, the voices will differ greatly from the eager voice of young George Ruth to the wise, authoritative voice of Brother Matthias, to the energetic, rowdy cheer of the fans. In "Chicken Tricks," page 65, performers can greatly vary character tones. Ellie's attitude ranges from jaunty to angry to humble as the play progresses. Wanda, Winnie, and Mae reprimand, worry, and support throughout the text. Point this out to readers and help them experiment with different ways they can use voices to convey feelings and responses.

Connect with Phonics

Each play offers opportunities to extend phonics awareness. While reading, look for connections to the following phonics skills. Encourage performers to practice saying aloud specific words and lines of dialogue until they master the skills you wish to target, such as:

Letter-Sound Relationships

* blends and digraphs
* high-frequency words
* vowel sounds
* word families
* rhyme

Word Structure

* compound words
* contractions
* homonyms
* plurals
* prefixes and suffixes
* syllabication

Manipulating the Script

Identify Key Features with Highlighting Tape

Have students use colorful highlighting tape to flag difficult words or those previously introduced. Point out these words before students read. Then deepen students' commitment to the text by inviting each student to highlight words they found challenging when they read through the script the first time—words they may need extra help decoding or defining.

Distinguish Lines of Dialogue

Encourage each student to use a highlighting marker in a specific color to identify the line(s) of dialogue their character(s) will be required to say. This color coding can help readers anticipate and prepare for their upcoming lines.

Enhancing the Readers Theater Experience

Encourage Teamwork

Encourage readers to pay attention not only to their own lines but to the lines of their fellow performers. Reading along while others speak their lines will promote fluent reading and will ensure that each performer is ready when his or her turn comes along.

Cast Several Teams of Performers

Allow one group of students to perform a play twice while all classmates follow along in their own copies of the script. Then ask a second group to perform the same play, again two times, while classmates read along. By the time a third group has performed, many students will be reading through the script with little effort. (Note: Because the varied cast members will bring their own interpretation and characteristics to the performance, seeing the play multiple times can also demonstrate various ways to interpret, present, and respond to the written word.)

To Ensure Involvement, Create Parts for Groups of Students

In plays such as "Chicken Tricks," page 65, and "Polly Learns to Swim," page 48, opportunities exist for groups of students to perform in choral roles. For example, although Ellie, Wanda, Mae, and Winnie carry the lead roles in "Chicken Tricks," the flock as a whole can make noise to protest the tricks Ellie plays by squawking, ruffling feathers, and sounding an emergency alert. Invite students to add these touches to the plays, writing them into the scripts beforehand and following along with the play rather than simply observing it.

Try Understudies . . . and Then Switch Roles

Cast students in lead roles and choose an understudy for each part. As in any theatrical performance, the role of the understudy is to familiarize him/herself with the character's lines in the event that the lead cannot perform for any reason. After several successful performances, switch roles and let the understudies play the lead parts.

Involve the Audience

Use Readers Theater to strengthen listening skills. After children perform, have them ask questions of their audience regarding the plot of the play and aspects of the presentation they especially liked, such as a character's use of expression or timing. Encourage the audience to state positive responses to the play and its performers, citing specific examples of actions or attitudes that helped them enjoy and understand the play more deeply, such as *I laughed when Jumping Joe asked "Am I good or what?" because he seemed so sure of himself!* or *I felt like what happened in the play was real, because the performers said their lines as if they were really the characters.* If warranted, invite viewers to offer the performers helpful suggestions to ensure a smoother or more meaningful performance in the future.

Boost Comprehension

After children perform, invite classmates to interview the performers in character, asking them to explain the reasons behind his or her actions in the play (for example, *Ellie, why did you leave the barn and run out into the field? How did you feel when you saw the fox running after you?* and *Wanda, how did you feel when Ellie wouldn't stop playing tricks? Did your feelings change when she was in danger out in the field? Why did you feel that way?*). To deepen comprehension, you may want to ask specific questions as if the play is a story, encouraging children to discuss the different personalities of the characters and what words or actions demonstrated their feelings, attitudes, or reactions.

Celebrate Success

Readers Theater offers powerful opportunities to boost confidence and improve skills in listening and speaking. Be sure to reward performers and listeners for advances in these areas. Note aloud when children have made particularly strong contributions to the play or when a child makes an insightful comment about the content or concept of a play.

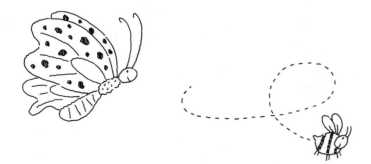

Resources for Reading Fluency, Comprehension, and Readers Theater

Armbruster, Bonnie B., Fran Lehr, and Jean Osborn. *Put Reading First: The Research Building Blocks for Teaching Children to Read.* (Center for the Improvement of Early Reading Achievement and the National Institute for Literacy. Office of Educational Research and Improvement, U.S. Department of Education, 2001)

Blevins, Wiley. *Building Fluency: Lessons and Strategies for Reading Success.* New York: Scholastic, 2001a.*

Blevins, Wiley. *Teaching Phonics and Word Study.* New York: Scholastic, 2001b.

Carrick, Lila. "Internet Resources for Conducting Readers Theatre." *Reading Online,* 5(1) http://www.readingonline.org/electronic/carrick

Clay, Marie M. *Becoming Literate: The Construction of Inner Control.* Portsmouth, NH: Heinemann, 1991.

Cunningham, Patricia M. and Richard L. Allington. *Classrooms That Work: They Can ALL Read and Write.* New York: Pearson Education, 2003.

Cunningham, Patricia, Dorothy P. Hall, and Cheryl M. Sigmon. *The Teacher's Guide to the Four Blocks.* Greensboro, NC: Carson-Dellosa, 1999.

Fiderer, Adele. 35 *Rubrics & Checklists to Assess Reading and Writing.* New York: Scholastic, 1998.

Fiderer, Adele. *40 Rubrics & Checklists to Assess Reading and Writing.* New York: Scholastic, 1999.

Fluency Formula: Grades 1–6. New York: Scholastic, 2003.*

Fountas, Irene C. and Gay Su Pinnell. *Guiding Readers and Writers.* Portsmouth, NH: Heinemann, 2001.

Fresch, Mary Jo and Aileen Wheaton. *Teaching and Assessing Spelling.* New York: Scholastic, 2002.

Harris, A. J. and M. D. Jacobson. *Basic Reading Vocabularies.* New York: Macmillan, 1982.

Heilman, Arthur W. *Phonics in Perspective.* Upper Saddle River, NJ: Pearson Education, 2002.

Kieff, Judith. "Revisiting the Read-Aloud." *Childhood Education.* Volume 80, No. 1, p. 28.

Lyon, G. R., J. M. Fletcher, S. E. Shaywitz, B. A. Shaywitz, J. K. Torgesen, F. B. Wood, A. Shulte, and R. Olson. "Rethinking Learning Disabilities." In C. E. Finn, R. A. J. Rotherham, and C. R. Hokanson (Eds.), *Rethinking Special Education for a New Century.* Washington, D.C.: Thomas B. Fordham Foundation & Progressive Policy Institute, 2001, pp. 259–287.

Lyon, G. Reid. "Why Reading Is Not a Natural Process." *Educational Leadership*, Volume 55, No. 6 (March 1998): pp. 14–18.

Lyon, G. Reid and Vinita Chhabra. "The Science of Reading Research." *Educational Leadership*, Volume 61, No. 6 (March 2004): pp. 12–17.

Northwest Territories Literacy Council. "Celebrate Literacy in the NWT: Readers Theatre." Abstract. http://www.nwt.literacy.ca/famlit/howtokit/theatre/2.htm

Pennington, Mark. *Better Spelling in 5 Minutes a Day.* Roseville, CA: Prima Publishing, 2001.

Pinnell, Gay Su and Patricia L. Scharer. *Teaching for Comprehension in Reading.* New York: Scholastic, 2003.*

Rasinski, Timothy. "Creating Fluent Readers." *Educational Leadership*, Volume 61, No. 6 (March 2004): pp. 46–51.

Rasinski, Timothy V. *3-Minute Reading Assessments: Word Recognition, Fluency, and Comprehension, Grades 1–4.* New York: Scholastic, 2005.

Rasinski, Timothy V. *The Fluent Reader*. New York: Scholastic, 2003.*

Shepard, Aaron. *Readers on Stage*. WA: Shepard Publications, 2004.

Tomlinson, Carol Ann. *The Differentiated Classroom*. Alexandria, VA: ASCD, 1999.

Torgesen, J. K. "The Prevention of Reading Difficulties." *Journal of School Psychology*, Volume 40, Issue 1, pp. 7–26.

Wagstaff, Janiel M. *Teaching Reading and Writing with Word Walls*. New York: Scholastic, 1999.

White, Sheida. "Listening to Children Read Aloud: Oral Fluency." *NAEP Facts*, National Center for Education Statistics. Volume 1, Number 1.

Worthy, Jo and Karen Broaddus. "Fluency Beyond the Primary Grades: From Group Performance to Silent, Independent Reading." *The Reading Teacher*, Volume 55, No. 4, pp. 334–343.

Worthy, Jo and Kathryn Prater. "I Thought About It All Night: Readers Theatre for Reading Fluency and Motivation (The Intermediate Grades)." *The Reading Teacher*, Volume 56, No. 3 (November 2002): p. 294.

Yopp, Hallie Kay and Ruth Helen Yopp. "Supporting Phonemic Awareness Development in the Classroom." *The Reading Teacher*, Volume 54, No. 2 (October 2000): pp. 130–143.

---

* This resource includes samples and/or examples of phrase-cued text.

Three Nice Mice

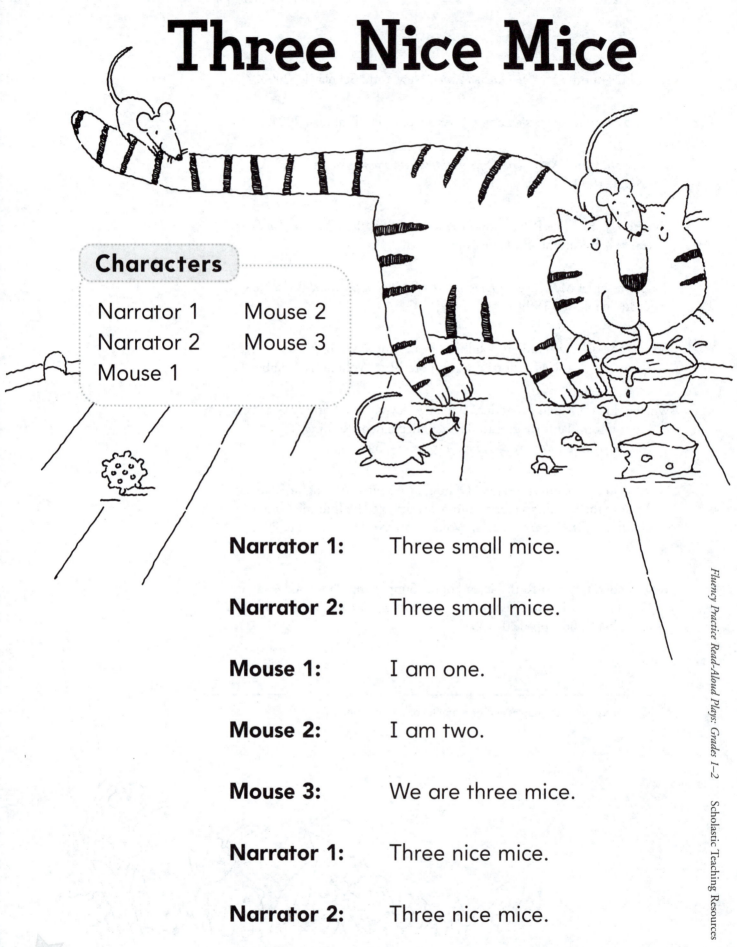

Characters

Narrator 1   Mouse 2
Narrator 2   Mouse 3
Mouse 1

Narrator 1:   Three small mice.

Narrator 2:   Three small mice.

Mouse 1:   I am one.

Mouse 2:   I am two.

Mouse 3:   We are three mice.

Narrator 1:   Three nice mice.

Narrator 2:   Three nice mice.

Fluency Practice Read-Aloud Plays: Grades 1–2 • Scholastic Teaching Resources

Mouse 1:   We help out.

Mouse 2:   We take turns.

Mouse 3:   We are nice.

Narrator 1:   One big cat.

Narrator 2:   One big cat.

Mouse 1:   We are small.

Mouse 2:   He is tall.

Mouse 3:   One big cat.

Mouse 1:   Here, big cat.

Mouse 2:   Here, big cat.

Mouse 3:   Sip our milk.

Mouse 1:	Eat our cheese.
Mouse 2:	Here, big cat.
Narrator 1:	Cat and mice.
Narrator 2:	Cat and mice.
Mouse 1:	Three and one.
Mouse 2:	This is fun!
Mouse 3:	Cat and mice.

 THE END

Who Needs a Fan?

Characters

Narrator
Dan
Nan
Jan

Narrator: The sun came out.
And out went Dan.

Dan: The sun is bright.
We'll get a tan!

Nan: It's hot out here.
We need a fan.

Jan: A fan out here?
I have a plan.

Dan: What is it, Jan?
What is your plan?

Jan: Can you feel wind?

Nan: Why, yes. I can!

Jan: We do not need to use a fan.
The wind can help us out.

Nan: It can?

Narrator: Jan held a kite.
She ran and ran.

Dan: The kite is high.
Keep running, Jan!

Fluency Practice Read-Aloud Plays: Grades 1–2

Scholastic Teaching Resources

Jan:	I will! I will keep running, Dan!
Nan:	We have the wind. Who needs a fan?
Dan:	It's windy here.
Nan:	Yes! Windy, Dan!
Jan:	Let's stay out here all day.
Dan and Nan:	Good plan!

❋ THE END ❋

Bear Cub Comes Home

Characters

Narrator   Bird
Bear Cub   Fish
Fox   Mother Bear
Pig

Narrator: A bear cub went for a walk.
                   He walked far from his home.

Bear Cub: It's getting late.
                   I must go home.
                   But where is my home?

Fluency Practice Read-Aloud Plays: Grades 1–2   Scholastic Teaching Resources

Narrator:	The little bear met a fox.
Bear Cub:	Who are you? Where is your home?
Fox:	I am a fox. I live in a den.
Narrator:	The little cub walked on. He met a pig.
Bear Cub:	Who are you? Where is your home?
Pig:	I am a pig. I live in a pen.
Bear Cub:	The fox lives in a den. The pig lives in a pen.
Narrator:	The cub walked on. He met a bird.
Bear Cub:	Who are you? Where is your home?

Bird: I am a bird.
                   I live in a tree.

Narrator: Now the little bear walked
                   a long, long way.
                   He met a fish.

Bear Cub: Who are you?
                   Where is your home?

Fish: I am a fish.
                   I live in the sea.

Bear Cub: The bird lives in a tree.
                   The fish lives in the sea.
                   They each know where to be.
                   Where is a home for me?

Narrator: The little cub walked and walked.
                   He came to a forest.

Bear Cub: I am very sleepy.
                   I will lie down and rest.
                   I will look for my home tomorrow.

Narrator: Just then, a big bear came along.

Fluency Practice Read-Aloud Plays: Grades 1–2   Scholastic Teaching Resources

Mother Bear: My little cub!
Where have you been?

Bear Cub: I have been trying to find home!

Mother Bear: What do you mean?

Bear Cub: The fox lives in a den.
The pig lives in a pen.
The bird lives in a tree.
The fish lives in the sea.
Where is a home for me?

Mother Bear: You are a bear.
You live in the woods.
You are my cub.
And you are home.

❊ THE END ❊

The Last Apple

Fluency Practice Read-Aloud Plays: Grades 1–2
Scholastic Teaching Resources

Characters

Narrator	Squirrel
Apple	Boy
Bird	Mother

Narrator: It is a cold fall day.

Apple: No more apples on my tree.
Every one is gone but me.

Bird: Where did all the apples go?

Apple: They have fallen.
Look below!

Bird: I see apples everywhere!

Apple: I wish I were way down there.

Squirrel: That is a long way to fall.

Apple: You are right.
This tree is tall.

Bird: Oh! A child has climbed this tree.

Squirrel: I must run.
He won't catch me!

Bird: It is time for me to fly.

Apple: Look!
This boy is up so high!

Boy: Mom! Look up!
See what I've found.
It's an apple, red and round.

Mother: Stop now!
You are up too high!

Boy: I am just below the sky!

Mother: Take the apple.
Hurry now.

Boy: I will come back down somehow.

Apple: Now I will not drop at all.

Boy: I will hold you.
You won't fall.
You are coming home with me.

Apple: Good-bye!
Good-bye, apple tree!

❆ THE END ❆

Fluency Practice Read-Aloud Plays: Grades 1–2   Scholastic Teaching Resources

The Sun Will Come

Characters

Narrator 1   Narrator 2
Mouse   Wind

Narrator 1:   A little mouse sat on the grass.

Mouse: It is dark, and I am cold.
I want to see the sun.

Narrator 2:   A soft wind blew.

Wind: Look, little mouse!
The moon has come out.
Its light is soft and pretty.

Mouse: The moon gives light,
but it is not warm.
I want to see the sun.

Wind: Wait, little one.
The sun will come.
The sun will come.

Narrator 1:   Time went by.

Mouse: It is still dark.
I am still cold.
I want to see the sun.

Narrator 2:   The wind pushed the clouds
from the sky.

Wind: Look, little mouse!
Now you can see lots of stars.

Mouse: The stars do not warm me.
They are too tiny
to give me much light.
I want to see the sun.

Fluency Practice Read-Aloud Plays: Grades 1–2 Scholastic Teaching Resources

| **Wind:** | Wait, little one.
The sun will come.
The sun will come. |
| **Narrator 1:** | The mouse lay down
on a bed of leaves. |
| **Mouse:** | I will rest here
and wait for the sun. |
| **Narrator 2:** | The mouse fell asleep. |
| **Wind:** | Mouse! It is morning!
Wake up! Wake up! |
| **Mouse:** | My face feels warm. |
| **Wind:** | Open your eyes, little mouse. |
| **Mouse:** | I see bright light.
The sun has come!
The sun has come! |

 THE END

I'm First!

Characters

Narrator	Anna
Lulu	Mr. Ross
Evan	

Narrator:	Lulu liked to be first.
Lulu:	I'm first on the slide!
Evan:	Okay, Lulu.
Lulu:	I'm first to jump rope!

Fluency Practice Read-Aloud Plays: Grades 1–2 • Scholastic Teaching Resources

Anna: Okay, Lulu.

Lulu: I'm first in the bus line!

Evan: You're always first, Lulu.

Lulu: I like to be first.

Narrator: Then one day, Lulu's class went for a walk.

Mr. Ross: Today, we're going to walk in the woods!

Lulu: I'm first in line!

Narrator: Lulu walked out the door. The class walked behind her.

Lulu: Here we go!

Mr. Ross: Stop when you get to the woods, Lulu.

Lulu: I know the way, Mr. Ross!

Anna:	Slow down, Lulu! You're walking too fast.
Evan:	Wait for us!
Narrator:	Lulu did not slow down. She walked into the woods.
Lulu:	I'll be the first to find pretty leaves!
Narrator:	Lulu picked up two yellow leaves.
Lulu:	Look what I found!
Narrator:	Lulu turned around. No one was there. Lulu felt scared.
Lulu:	I must have gone the wrong way. I'll walk over here.
Narrator:	Lulu could not find her friends. She kept walking.
Lulu:	Help! Evan! Anna! I'm lost!

Fluency Practice Read-Aloud Plays: Grades 1–2 Scholastic Teaching Resources

Mr. Ross: Lulu! There you are!
I told you not to go
into the woods.

Lulu: I wanted to be first.

Mr. Ross: You were first.
But you got lost, too.

Lulu: I'm sorry, Mr. Ross.
May I walk with Anna and Evan?

Anna: Then you won't be first.

Lulu: I don't want to be first now.
I just want to be with my friends.

✳ THE END ✳

Live at the Number Games

Characters

Fred Fun   Running Ray
Jumping Joe   TV Man
Bowling Beth

Fred Fun: Hi! We're here LIVE
at the number games!
I'm your host, Fred Fun.

Jumping Joe: Fred! Over here!

Fred Fun: It's Jumping Joe!

Jumping Joe: I am about to jump over this hole in the sand.

Fred Fun: That hole is five feet long! Can you jump that far?

Jumping Joe: Watch me!

(*Joe jumps.*)

Fred Fun: Wow! That was some jump!

Jumping Joe: I jumped five feet! Am I good or what?

Bowling Beth: Fred! Over here!

Fred Fun: It's Bowling Beth!

Bowling Beth: I am about to tip over ten pins with one ball.

Fred Fun: Can you do that?

Bowling Beth: Watch me!

(*She rolls the ball. Ten pins fall.*)

Fred Fun: Wow! You did it!

Bowling Beth: Ten pins!
Am I good or what?

Running Ray: Fred! Over here!

Fred Fun: It's Running Ray!

Running Ray: I am about to run one mile
in seven minutes.

Fred Fun: Can you run that fast?

Running Ray: Watch me!

(*He runs and runs.*)

Fred Fun: You did it!

Running Ray: Seven minutes!
Am I good or what?

Fluency Practice Read-Aloud Plays: Grades 1–2   Scholastic Teaching Resources

TV Man:	Fred Fun! Over here!
Fred Fun:	It's my boss!
TV Man:	We have two seconds left in our show. You need to say good-bye, Fred.
Fred Fun:	Well, this ends our time at the Number Games! Tune in next week when we go to the Letter Limbo!

 THE END

Polly Learns to Swim

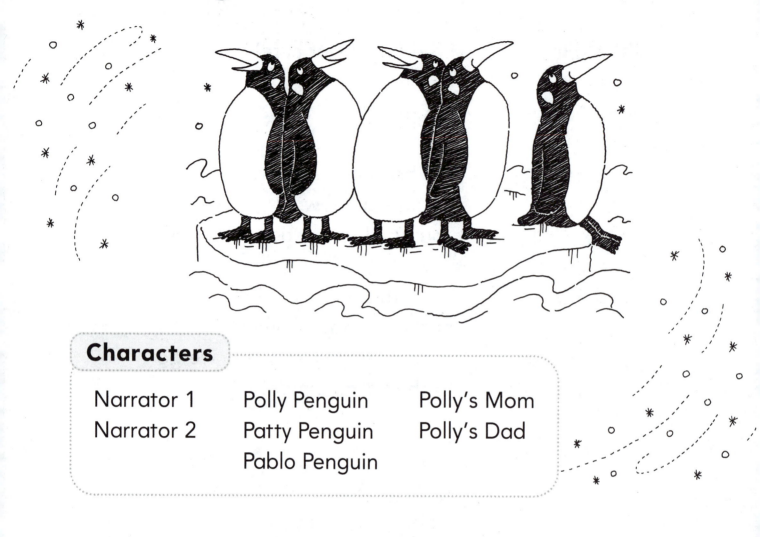

Characters

Narrator 1	Polly Penguin	Polly's Mom
Narrator 2	Patty Penguin	Polly's Dad
	Pablo Penguin	

Narrator 1: One day, five penguins stood by the sea.

Narrator 2: Waves splashed their feet.

Polly Penguin: This water is cold!

Patty Penguin: It feels colder than snow!

Pablo Penguin: I can't wait to swim!

Practice Read-Aloud Plays: Grades 1–2   Scholastic Teaching Resources

Polly Penguin:	I'm not going in without my mom and dad.
Narrator 1:	Polly turned around.
Narrator 2:	She walked over ice and snow.
Polly Penguin:	Mom! Dad!
Polly's Mom:	That sounds like Polly's cry. Do you see her?
Polly's Dad:	Here she comes now.
Polly Penguin:	The other chicks want to swim. But I'm scared.
Polly's Mom:	We'll take you swimming.
Polly's Dad:	We'll teach you how to find fish to eat.
Narrator 1:	Polly and her mom and dad walked to the water.
Polly Penguin:	The water is too cold!

Polly's Mom: Don't be afraid.

Polly's Dad: Your body is made for cold water. You have fat in your body to keep it warm.

Polly's Mom: You have feathers to keep you warm, too.

Polly Penguin: I don't know how to swim. What if I sink?

Polly's Mom: You won't sink. You'll see.

Narrator 2:   SPLASH!
Polly's mom and dad
went under the water.

Narrator 1:   SPLASH!
Polly went under
for the very first time.

Narrator 2:   Polly's body knew what to do.

Narrator 1:   Her flippers pushed her through the water.

Fluency Practice Read-Aloud Plays: Grades 1–2   Scholastic Teaching Resources

Polly Penguin:	I'm swimming!
Narrator 2:	Polly swam to the top of the water.
Polly Penguin:	I did it! I did it!
Narrator 1:	Polly saw her friends out in the waves.
Polly Penguin:	I did it! I'm swimming!
Patty Penguin:	We'll race you to the rocks!
Polly Penguin:	Let's go!
Polly's Mom:	Well, what are we waiting for?
Polly's Dad:	I'll race you to the rocks!

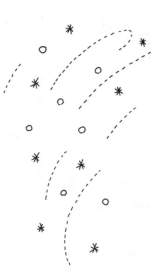

THE END

Babe Ruth

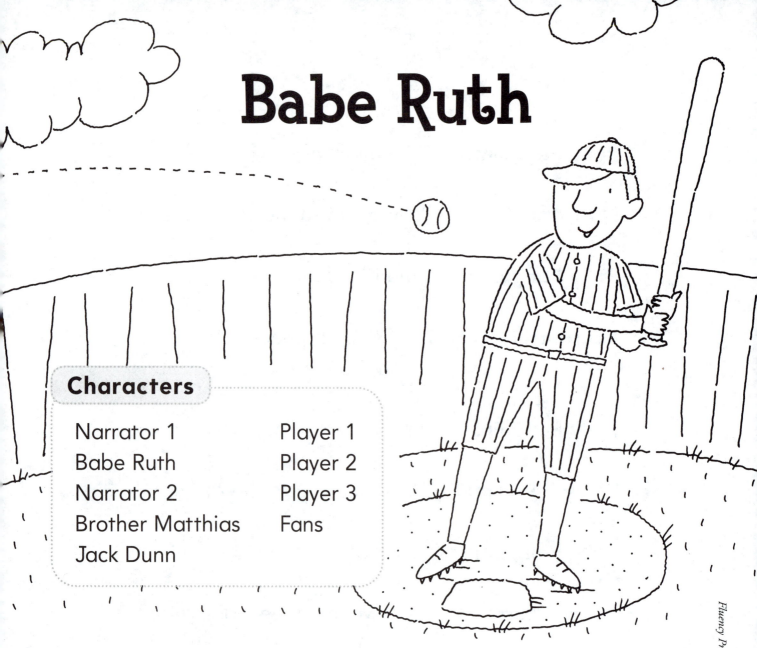

Characters

Narrator 1   Player 1
Babe Ruth   Player 2
Narrator 2   Player 3
Brother Matthias   Fans
Jack Dunn

Narrator 1:	More than 100 years ago, George Ruth was seven years old. He lived at a school for boys.
Babe Ruth:	My life is not fun. There is nothing to do.
Narrator 2:	One of his teachers had an idea.

Fluency Practice Read-Aloud Plays: Grades 1–2   Scholastic Teaching Resources

Brother Matthias:	Come here, George. Hold this bat.
Babe Ruth:	What is it for?
Brother Matthias:	I will throw a ball to you. Hit it with the bat.
Babe Ruth:	What if I miss?
Brother Matthias:	Just try.
Narrator 1:	George hit the ball.
Brother Matthias:	That was some hit! That ball went over my head!
Babe Ruth:	Let's do it again!
Narrator 2:	George hit the ball again.
Brother Matthias:	You are good at this game!
Narrator 1:	George loved to hit the ball. He loved to throw and catch. He wanted to play ball every day.

Narrator 2:   Twelve years went by.
George was 19 years old.
A man came to see him.

Jack Dunn: My name is Jack Dunn.
I've seen you play,
and you're really good.
I want you to join my team.
I will pay you well.

Narrator 1:   George played
on Jack Dunn's team.
The fans and players loved him.

Player 1:   He hits the ball hard!

Player 2:   He throws the ball fast!

Player 3:   He is so young!
Let's call him Babe!

Fans: Babe Ruth!
Babe Ruth!
Babe Ruth!

Chicken Tricks

Characters

Narrator	Mae
Ellie	Winnie
Wanda	

Narrator:	Once there lived a chicken who liked to play tricks.
Ellie:	Hey, Wanda! I laid ten eggs today!
Wanda:	Chickens don't lay that many eggs in one day!
Ellie:	Well, I did. Come and see.

Wanda:	(*counting*) That's ten eggs all right! How did you do it?
Mae and Winnie:	Our eggs are gone! Other hens are missing theirs, too!
Ellie:	Ha! Ha! I fooled you, Wanda! Only one egg is mine!
Mae and Winnie:	(*crossly*) Give us back our eggs, Ellie.
Narrator:	Later that day, Ellie locked the henhouse.
Wanda:	Ellie, open this door! Let us out!
Ellie:	(*laughing*) The wind is holding the door shut!
Narrator:	That night, Wanda spoke to Ellie.
Wanda:	Ellie, you must stop playing tricks.

Fluency Practice Read-Aloud Plays: Grades 1–2 Scholastic Teaching Resources

Ellie:	I'm just having fun, Wanda.
Wanda:	Well, no one else is. You need to stop.
Ellie:	(*crossly*) What I need is to get out of here.
Narrator:	Ellie stepped through a hole in the fence.
Wanda:	You're going into the field? At night?
Mae:	You could get eaten by a fox!
Winnie:	Don't give her any ideas. She'll just play more tricks.
Narrator:	Wanda, Mae, and Winnie walked back to the henhouse. Just then, Ellie saw a fox.
Ellie:	(*shouting*) Fox on the farm! Fox on the farm!
Winnie:	See? What did I tell you? Ellie is playing tricks again.

Ellie: (*shouting*) Fox on the farm! Help! Help!

Wanda: Ellie sounds scared.
We'd better see what's going on.

Narrator: The three hens stepped out
of the henhouse. They saw Ellie
running around in the field.
Right behind her ran a big red fox.

Mae: Ellie! Come in through here! Hurry!

Narrator: Ellie raced through the hole in the fence.
Mae and Winnie slid a board across
the hole to keep out the fox.

Ellie: Thank you! Thank you! You saved my life!

Wanda: We didn't believe you at first.

Ellie: I'm lucky that you listened this last time.

Wanda: Last time? Does this mean you're done
playing tricks?

Fluency Practice Read-Aloud Plays: Grades 1–2   Scholastic Teaching Resources

Ellie:	It will be hard, but I'll try.
Narrator:	Wanda, Mae, and Winnie walked toward the henhouse.
Ellie:	Wait! Let me go in first! I put rocks in your beds. I need to get them out!
Wanda:	(*shaking her head*) Ellie, you're one of a kind.

 THE END

Cats Care for Their Kittens

Characters

Emma
Toby
Sara
Emma's Mom
Narrator

Emma:	Toby! Sara! Come see! My cat Missy had six kittens!
Toby:	Six kittens!
Sara:	They are so small!
Emma:	Missy won't let us pick them up. She wants to take care of them.

Sara:	Why is she licking them?
Emma's Mom:	She's cleaning them. She'll do that until they are big enough to do it on their own.
Emma:	Mom says Missy makes milk for her kittens to drink.
Emma's Mom:	Kittens can't eat when they are so little. They can only drink.
Toby:	I want to come back when the kittens are bigger.
Sara:	I want to hold them!
Narrator:	Four weeks go by.
Emma:	Look at the kittens!
Toby:	They are so much bigger!
Sara:	Look! That one is running out of the room!

Toby: Missy's running after it.
Let's go!

Sara: Emma! Missy is going
to bite the kitten!

Emma: She's not biting, Sara.
She's picking up the kitten
with her mouth.

Sara: Do the kittens still drink
Missy's milk?

Emma: Some of the time.
Now we give the kittens
food to eat, too.

Toby: You're taking good care
of the kittens, Emma.

Emma: Missy's doing most of the work!

Narrator: Four more weeks pass.

Toby: Where are the kittens, Emma?

Fluency Practice Read-Aloud Plays: Grades 1–2 Scholastic Teaching Resources

Emma: They have gone to new homes.
Missy does not need
to care for them now.
They can clean themselves
and eat on their own.

Sara: Oh! I was hoping we could keep one.

Emma: I know. Your mom came over today.

Sara: Why?

Emma: She wanted the last kitten in a good home.
Yours!

(*Emma hands Sara the kitten.*)

Sara: Wow! Our own kitten!
Thank you, Emma!

(*Toby pets Missy.*)

Toby: And thanks to Missy.
She took good care of her kittens!

 THE END

Hide and Go Seek!

Characters

Narrator 1
Narrator 2
Sue Stick Bug
Fred Frog
Suki Squirrel
Mike Mouse
Dan Deer

Narrator 1:   One summer day
in the bright yellow sun,
five little friends played
a game just for fun.

Narrator 2:   They played a game they called
Hide and Go Seek.

Sue Stick Bug: Dan, you start counting.
We'll hide. Don't you peek!

Narrator 1:   Dan counted quickly.
His friends ran to hide.

Narrator 2:   There were so many
great places outside!

Fred Frog: He'll never find me,
for I am a frog.
My skin is as green
as the moss on this log.

Sue Stick Bug: My body is brown.
It is long and so thin!
Dan won't see me
on this stick. I will win!

Suki Squirrel: My fur is gray
like the bark of a tree.
I'll climb up a tree trunk.
He'll never find me!

Mike Mouse: My fur is the color of dirt.
It is brown.
Dan won't find me
in these leaves that fell down.

Narrator 1: Dan finished counting
and looked all around.
He saw the tip of a tail
on the ground.

Dan Deer: Mike, I have found you.
Your long tail I see.
Come out! Come out!
Now you can help me!

Mike Mouse: Something just moved on that log!
Did you see?

Dan Deer: That someone has to be Fred!

Mike Mouse: I agree!

Fred Frog: I will come help you
now that you've found me.
Look! Is that Suki's
long tail that I see?

Mike Mouse: Yes, it is Suki.
She's high in the air.
Now that she moved,
I can see her up there.

Fluency Practice Read-Aloud Plays: Grades 1–2   Scholastic Teaching Resources

Fred Frog: Now there's just one of us hiding.
It's Sue!

Dan Deer: If I were a stick bug,
then what would I do?

Suki Squirrel: One time, Sue showed me
her favorite trick.
When she sits still,
she looks just like a stick!

Fred Frog: There's a long branch.
That might give us a clue.
Hey, look! It's moving!

Dan Deer: I knew it! It's Sue!

Mike Mouse: This is the end
of our game for today.
Tomorrow, I know
a new game we can play.
You'll close your eyes.
You may not even peek.
I'll make a noise.

Sue Stick Bug: We'll play Hide and Go Squeak!

 THE END ❊

Little Puppy

ruff! ruff! ruff! ruff! ruff!

Characters

Narrator 1	Puppy
Narrator 2	Eve
Jay	Sal

Narrator 1: In an itty-bitty city lived
a very pretty pup.

Narrator 2: She was really very tiny.
Yet no one could pick her up.

Jay: I would really like to hold you!
I will give you this big bone.

Narrator 1: But the puppy would not listen.

Fluency Practice Read-Aloud Plays: Grades 1–2   Scholastic Teaching Resources

Puppy:	Ruff! Ruff! Ruff! Leave me alone!
Eve:	Little puppy, let me hold you. I will give you food to eat.
Narrator 2:	But the puppy would not listen.
Puppy:	Ruff! Ruff! Ruff! I want no treat.
Sal:	Little puppy, let me hold you. I will make you a soft bed.
Narrator 1:	But the puppy would not listen.
Puppy:	Ruff! Ruff! Ruff!
Narrator 2:	The puppy said.
Jay, Eve, and Sal:	What a puppy!
Narrator 1:	Said the children.

Jay, Eve, and Sal:	What a puppy!
Narrator 2:	They said twice.
Jay:	She won't even let us pet her!
Eve:	Our new puppy is not nice.
Sal:	Look! Here comes another puppy!
Jay:	What will our new puppy do?
Eve:	Look! Our puppy wags her tail now!
Sal:	And the other pup wags, too!
Jay:	Maybe our pup felt unhappy.
Eve:	She just missed her puppy friends!
Sal:	Look! She let me pick her up!
Narrator 1:	And so this story ends.

❅ THE END ❅

Fluency Practice Read-Aloud Plays: Grades 1–2

Scholastic Teaching Resources